WHAT PEOPLE ARE ~~UNC~~ ~~GEMS~~

Paul Godin provides a timely and critical reminder that people are THE most precious and valuable resource on the planet, exponentially impacting not only the present but the future as we know it. It's not a question of whether we have influence, but HOW we are influencing. *Uncut Gems* will challenge you to lead on purpose with purpose and to see others discover, become, and live out the best versions of themselves.

—Jonathan Edwards
Director, Daybreak Leadership College

I'm thrilled to endorse Paul Godin's new book, *Uncut Gems*. Having worked closely with Paul, I can attest to the profound impact he has had on unlocking the potential of those around him. Our friendship has been a journey of shared challenges and insightful conversations, making Paul not just a colleague but a trusted voice of wisdom in these areas.

Uncut Gems is a valuable guide that addresses the crucial question of how we can discover, develop, and deploy the potential within our circles. Paul's depth of experience and thoughtful exploration of intentionality sets this book apart. It goes beyond theory, confronting the prevalent issue of neglecting human capital and demanding accountability from leaders.

As someone who has witnessed Paul's commitment to uplifting others, I wholeheartedly endorse *Uncut Gems* as a transformative resource for anyone involved in human development. This book reflects not only Paul's expertise but also his genuine passion for helping individuals find their best place to shine.

—Caleb Womack
Director of Operations, Regency Supply

With the unquestioned need for more effective leaders everywhere, Paul Godin resolves to meet the challenge with a unique passion, pragmatism, and experience. During the twenty-five years of our friendship, he has consistently and selflessly refined numerous uncut gems to produce persevering leaders with vision and relevant skills for implementation. *Uncut Gems* reveals his substantial knowledge and experience in ways that will undoubtedly enhance your development of potential leaders.

—Dave Metsker
Leadership Development Network

Since the first time I met Paul Godin, he has been searching for and seeking individuals to invest in with everything he has. Without a doubt, this investment has led to multi-generational life changes that will forever impact the family trees of many. Without leaders like Paul, people would never have a chance to be refined into a better version of themselves and make changes that have a positive impact on the world around us. Undoubtedly, I can recount many instances where Paul and his wife, Alisha, have seen gifts/talents in individuals before they or anyone else around them could ever see them. I don't believe this is just a unique personality trait or characteristic, but rather a needed posture of habitual discipline to be replicated. I personally cannot think of anyone more fit to relay the processes, functionality, and heart behind investing in the human capital that we have at our fingertips already. With Paul's help, leaders will level up AND they will take everyone who is following with them.

—Dakota Severson
SGT, U.S. ARMY

The unapologetic spirit of Paul Godin doubles down in this guide designed to root out the intentionality and motivation behind the discipleship model. Paul presents a compelling case for the development of human capital within the context of organizational leadership in a way that both exposes the drivers behind why we lead, as well as what strategies are vital to produce enduring disciples. Paul has major cred with his insights about the commission of the called-out and the distinguished honor of being a mentor-discipler. As someone who has been deeply impacted by his passionate methodology in real time, I am convinced that his manner of plainspeak will resonate with and challenge you on a deeply personal level.

—Rev. Bruce Allan

I have known Paul Godin for almost as long as I can remember and I am all the better for it. He has taught and modeled to me the things in this book, both in a work setting as well as in his day-to-day life. In our time together, I have seen him intentionally work to grow in his leadership knowledge, and then immediately turn around and share that knowledge with others. Paul has my strong endorsement for his book *Uncut Gems*. Based on the things he has personally taught and modeled to me, I know without a doubt that what he has to share will help you the same way it has helped me.

—Jacob Coffey
Technical Director, Lifehouse

From day one, as a manager in our workplace, Paul wanted to invest in me. He took the time weekly to pour into me and help develop me in my professional career. For that, I am beyond thankful. This was genuinely the case with everyone he came into contact with. He prioritized relationships, walking out the method outlined in this book. In fact, Paul would talk to me about the Diamond Miner ideology often at work. His book reinforces this ideology—when you're in the right role, poured into, and given an opportunity to flourish, you will. He encouraged me to look for those diamonds in the rough and give them my best.

—Glenn Elmore
Account Manager, Regency Supply

I have known Paul for the past twelve years both professionally and personally, and I can attest he is a thoughtful and insightful guy with a great lens into seeing both sides of any issue without compromising his own values. Paul was instrumental in our ringtone and video start-up business over a decade ago when it was in its infancy. Paul worked as "Head of Digital Media and Entertainment" for Rackspace, and he was always knowledgeable and available, not to mention extremely friendly, which was how our friendship began. In addition to knowing his product and his profession, he was PARAMOUNT in providing some very valuable feedback as a person and a citizen. I asked for his honest opinion, and he felt that some of my content would not be appropriate for some viewers, and he cogently pointed out some possible insensitivities that I had not even seen. I do not need to go into specifics, but his wise advice saved me from making a permanent bad decision that could not be "undone." Paul's sensitivity "for the little guy" made me reevaluate my video, and I made something much less offensive. Paul is not a prude. Paul is a peacemaker, and he always has shown tremendous equanimity. He was always a calm voice on the other end of the customer service line and that is extremely unusual these days. I was extremely impressed and remember thinking he would be a great team leader somewhere. On a personal level, he is a loyal and devoted family man and loves his community and university, and it doesn't hurt that he plays some pretty good John Denver-like songs on guitar. He is just an all-around outstanding and great guy, and that means he is great with ALL kinds of people from all walks of life. That was apparent in the way he treated me many years ago.

—Teddy Vardell
Vocal Talent, Voice Carousel and more

UNCUT
GEMS

DISCOVERING, DEVELOPING, AND DEPLOYING
THE DIAMONDS AROUND YOU

PAUL GODIN, M.A.

DREAM
RELEASER
PUBLISHING

Dedication
To the original Diamond Miner, Jesus Christ,
and to my wife, my children and grandson,
my faith community, and all the diamond
miners who saw value in me and taught me
to see the value in others, "Thank You."

CONTENTS

FOREWORD

I was given the great honor of introducing you readers to the author of this book, and my father, Paul Godin. Because I am his eldest daughter, I have seen him through many chapters of life. Yes, he has a master's in strategic leadership, but besides his academics, there are countless other reasons why he is uniquely qualified to share this leadership paradigm shift. My two siblings and I often joked that he was the male Barbie since he was never too prideful to risk failure and apply himself to learn an entirely new career path when the opportunity was given. Ambitious, studious, disciplined, strategic, intentional, and highly discerning are a few words to describe Paul Godin. Wherever there was a need that required him, he would rise to the occasion. When my mom wanted to homeschool, he would take on however many jobs necessary to provide that blessing for his family. When the schools in our area needed help, he showed up. When the community encouraged him to utilize his business expertise in a political setting, he didn't shy away from the challenge. When his kids were hurting for time with their father, he would take notice and make the time to take us out on a date or even stay up late after a long day to tend to our needs. One morning, I recall waking up before my father to thoughtfully pack a small suitcase of homework and toys to convince him to take me with him to work. I would limit the possibility of him saying no because I was completely ready to go and eagerly waiting at the end of our staircase with luggage full of things to occupy myself with. A child awaiting their father's approval is a vulnerable spot to be in. I didn't need him to entertain me, but to simply include me in his mundane day-to-day so that I would get to know more of him. Not only was he exceedingly pleased to take me to work, satisfying my love language of quality time, but he didn't ask me to continually keep to myself. Instead, he gave me a tour, showed me what he did, introduced me to coworkers, and made me feel that I had something to contribute. He taught me that I could ask, and when he could, he would give. He showed me that I didn't even have to stick to one career path; I could write a song, write a book, raise a family, pick up photography, and run in any lane that I chose. Even when I didn't believe I was capable, he did. Now, I don't believe I have met one person who is completely devoid of a fear of rejection, and that includes my father. What I do know is that he has successfully taught me by modeling it himself, that a fear of rejection from others should not permit self-rejection. Do not assume failure before you've let it play out, and even in the case that you do fail, your two steps back are a chance to start again from a place of better knowledge and experience than before your setback. This message has meant so much to me because I tend to naturally assume self-rejection. But how can I hold myself back from the right open doors in life when my dad has shown me how to courageously walk through them? How can I selfishly hide away from the world or squander the opportunity to multiply for others what I've been given when he has always pointed back to the God that so freely gives? In this book, you will find his passion for legacy, not only to equip you to teach your circles how to properly walk through the doors in front of them but also to recount the tried-and-true lessons to *their* circles. His message is compelling: what we have to give does not end with us but carries on from generation to generation. It is a compact and powerful read that will influence more than one area of your life. I believe you will find yourself coming back again and again, seeing things from an entirely new perspective. So, I ask that you please ruminate on these truths with the same measure of care that it was written, and without further ado ... *Uncut Gems.*

—Serena McDaniel

ACKNOWLEDGMENTS

Bruce Allan, thank you for your proofreading skills, your sense of humor, your ability to just "get it," and your constant encouragement. You are a wellspring of joy.

Megan Adelson, thank you for your endless curiosity and for asking me clarifying questions that helped me articulate my thoughts in a more concise manner. You held my hand and spurred me on until this book took a sensible shape.

Jesse Pratt, thank you for being an early adopter and seed investor so that this message could get out there. Your intellect and appetite for continual learning always makes for great dialogue. You are a loyal friend.

Serena McDaniel, thank you for tackling the foreword of this glorified toilet reader. I feel as though I'm listening to my own eulogy while I'm alive, and I'm humbled. Honestly, you have lived out the words in this book, and you continually elevate so many gems around you. Thank you for testing these theories. You are the ultimate R&D partner.

INTRODUCTION

I have witnessed in the home, in the marketplace, and in various expressions of faith communities, a problem that I cannot be silent about. I've wrestled with the timing and tone of this message, and I've found myself conflicted. Trying to find the softest, kindest wording that might still adequately convey the seriousness and urgency of what I've witnessed is no easy task. So, I will just speak plainly:

> *"A perpetual negligence has left the human capital (people) in our care, largely undiscovered, under-utilized, and/or underdeveloped for far too long."*

My motives in saying this are not to needlessly attack or nit-pick but to say: "Enough is enough!" I have seen this travesty go on and on, and I want to offer some solutions, some prescriptions even, to aid in rectifying this disturbing trend. I humbly submit the following chapters as a possibility for your and my continual consideration; a way of reasoning with our conscience and holding ourselves accountable to press forward with some level of action steps. I don't want to leave you with more information or some empty theories that don't actually move you. I don't want this to be just another book on your shelf. I want this to be your favorite toilet reader—the book that you keep coming back to and wrestling with—staring you down every time you have to use the bathroom. I want this to be the book that addresses a subject you simply cannot ignore any longer. In fact, I hope it becomes the book you share with all of your leader friends, and it becomes a textbook in your corporate onboarding process.

I acknowledge the very nature of this book's content and the challenges I present to leaders will lend themselves at times to being taken personally, and possibly cause you to write me off. Please don't do that. The truth of this message may sting a bit, but it should sting and lead you to change. Ultimately, this book isn't about me or my opinions. It is offered on behalf of those whose voice may not have the right audience or any audience at all. It is for the human capital in our care who deserve better from us. As you read this book, consider it from their perspective and I think you'll come to agree with me.

Some will justify this negligent trend as sheer ignorance, exclaiming, "No one ever taught me differently." Others will cry, "That takes too much work" or "That is too idealistic and unrealistic." Still, others will see all the facts, and the collateral damage that ensues when disregarded, and they will willfully choose to continue down a pathway that is prohibitive and ultimately destructive to their own family, business, and/or faith community. Ignorance? Ineptitude? Laziness? Stubbornness? Pride? These have never been and will never be acceptable excuses. They are not the characteristics of good leadership. No human capital should suffer at their hands.

While it may be easier to take offense and/or try to excuse away the information presented here as merely the author's opinion, I think somewhere deep down this book will strike a nerve with all readers, and it will force you, as it did myself, to look in the mirror and take personal ownership of our leadership decisions and the ensuing collateral from those choices. The fruit of our leadership choices is evident, factual, and measurable. Our leadership fruit is our human capital, and ultimately how they grow in their own maturity and contribution to society. Their very lives bear witness to the validity and credibility of our leadership efforts—our intentional investment in them.

When it comes to parenting, training our employees and/or direct reports, or working with volunteers in a not-for-profit and/or faith context, there are generally two schools of thought around developing the human capital in our care. One can either choose to "form it" or they can look to "filch it" from someone else who actually did the forming. In this book, I use the metaphor of a Diamond Miner and a Jewelry Thief to capture the differences in the ideology and methodology employed by these two paradigms of leadership thought. It is not meant to be an oversimplification by any means, but rather an easy way to self-assess our natural tendencies when it comes to developing our human capital and to be honest regarding the changes we may need to make. I acknowledge that some abdicate their role entirely, but I just add that to the Jewelry Thief's disposition.

My unapologetic goal for this book is to galvanize a significant portion of malleable leaders toward actual philosophical and behavioral change. I will compare and contrast the mindsets and actions of a Diamond Miner and Jewelry Thief to make my case. If you follow the five steps in the Diamond Mining process, you will begin to see potential where you didn't see it before; you will recognize the value and costly investment to bring forth that potential in another; you will gain insight into ways to develop with specificity; and you will come to terms with your motives behind it all. Lastly, you'll be able to assess with some urgency the need to not only begin in the first place but to continue the process indefinitely.

It goes without saying that there will always be some exceptions and/or variables to each person's story—more color and complexity that add differing perspectives. I'm not writing to wage an argument with each outlier. I simply want to take a pragmatic look and give a State of the Union on our current and woeful approach to the development of the human capital in our purview and ask that we work together to truly adjust our norm and begin to elevate those in our care. I believe we can all be Diamond Miners and help the diamonds around us find their best place to shine.

CHAPTER 1

SURVEYING
SEE THE WAY

I n the fall of 2018, after a four-year hiatus in Washington state, I returned to Texas to work alongside my friend of twenty-seven years, Ryan, for a second stint. When I left San Antonio, Texas, back in November of 2014, I actually left on Thanksgiving Day, missing out on our yearly tradition—the TURKEY BOWL! Somewhere along my drive north, I received a call from him lamenting that our beloved game was just not as fun as it had been the previous seven years. I suspect it's because we weren't together to talk our usual trash, and I wasn't there for him to whoop up on me. Turkey Bowl was our family's annual Thanksgiving Day tradition of flag football with extended friends and family who either lived in town or came in for the holiday. Young or old, male or female, all were welcome to participate in our amazing gridiron classic.

For years, the night before Turkey Bowl I would get the balls pumped up, the flags and belts sorted by color, I'd pull the end zone pylons out of storage, I'd sterilize some ref whistles, and then I'd set my outfit out next to the door. (Yes, I had a full outfit, because you have to dress for the job you want!) My outfit consisted of some combination of hunter orange and black, and Ryan would invariably wear some shade of puke green and yellow. To give a little context, Ryan and I were actually Oregon transplants to Texas. Every year we made our Texas Turkey

Bowl a very poor version of the historic Civil War—that is the rivalry game between our respective home state teams, the Oregon Ducks and the Oregon State Beavers. (Yes, we made all the Baylor Bears, Texas Longhorns, Texas A&M Aggies, and Texas Tech Red Raiders acquiesce to our home-state rivalry.)

It would be historically accurate to say that my friend and I had very different approaches to our Turkey Bowl games over the years. Ryan is decently athletic, highly competitive, and unwilling to go home to Thanksgiving dinner with a loss. He would stiff-arm his own grandmother to score a game-winning touchdown. As soon as Ryan showed up to the football field, he'd be eyeing the talent and scheming for how he was going to get bragging rights again.

Make no mistake, I wanted to win too, but I mainly wanted everyone on my team to have a good time. It required a lot of creativity because the athletic gene was limited in my own case, and in some of my friend groups, it skipped them entirely. On my teams of misfits and musicians, multiple people got a chance at QB. We would make up terribly executed trick plays and try to spread the ball around so that everyone got some holiday football action. Needless to say, our outfits were better than our on-field play!

The fall that I returned to Texas, Ryan asked me if we were going to do the Turkey Bowl. I figured we were too old and should simply referee, but he wanted to play, so I obliged. As word spread that the epic rivalry was back on, participants came out in full force, ready to create their own memories and become suburban legends.

Over the years, we actually had some decent talent come out, and Ryan loved to stack his Turkey Bowl team with them whenever possible. Knowing Ryan's tendencies to survey the fresh crop of recruits and grab for the obvious talent, I decided to play into that overconfidence and mess with him a bit. I actually began scripting a plan a couple of weeks prior to the game. You see, that year at church, I had met a former Division One QB (who played at the University of Miami and Baylor) and Ryan didn't know him yet. Leading up to the big game, I convinced Ryan's son, Jacob, and Ryan's son's friend, Ethan, to join my team, telling them I had a secret weapon, and promising them gridiron glory . . . or at least a chance to mess with dad.

When we got to the selection of our teams that brisk fall morning, I let Ryan take some of the best and most familiar talent. Great arms, sure hands, it didn't matter. I let him just pick away. I let Ryan believe his team had all the talent, but we knew two young soccer players in the lineup, and we had the inside knowledge that they were in superb shape and fast as lightning. Ryan passed on them. Things looked pretty lopsided and not in our favor, so to seal my perceived fate, and with a flair for the dramatic, I picked this no-name 6'3" guy in generic 1970s sweatpants. He looked like a tall Uncle Rico from Napoleon Dynamite.

When the game opened, Ryan expected me to play QB just like he does—to captain my team to victory. Instead, I deferred QB duty to this no-namer and told every one of those young guys to just run straight for the end zone, looking over their shoulders in exactly "3 Mississippi's." Upon the hike of the ball, the young guns fired off the line in a dead sprint for the end zone. The defense began shouting out "one Mississippi, two Mississippi, three Mississippi" and then they broke the line of scrimmage, menacingly pursuing our QB's flag. Like clockwork, "Uncle Rico" drew them in, then sidestepped the entire defensive rush, throwing a 70-yard dart downfield, over the outside shoulder of the receiver—TOUCHDOWN! After a defensive stop, we just went at it again. Our mystery QB threw 50-, 60-, 70-yard dimes to these kids who simply ran Hail Mary routes downfield, leaving the defense gassed and their own hands hurting because our QB put some heat on those passes. Touchdown! Touchdown! Touchdown! Their defense didn't know what hit them. We were killing Ryan's team, and it was awesome.

It didn't take long for Ryan and his team to realize they had misjudged the situation and this unknown individual. He was no ordinary player. The perfect spirals and passing precision were dead giveaways that he was a different caliber of player. Our QB was the most talented individual any of us had ever played with in our long-standing flag football game. The cries for a reshuffling of the teams to "make it competitive" were satisfactory enough. After a few laughs from the shock and awe we unleashed, we mixed it up and went back to sharing QB opportunities, silly trick plays, and just having a great time together.

When you look at the obvious talent and fail to investigate the potential in others, even when they're right under your nose, you might just miss out on that once-in-a-generation kind of talent.

LOOK BEYOND THE SURFACE

Sometimes what we see on the surface is an accurate picture of a person, but rarely is it the full picture. Most people hold their cards close to their chest and slowly with time begin to be more vulnerable and open themselves up to others. So on the surface, we may see attendance habits, work ethic, dress attire, various skills, vocabulary, sense of humor, and manner of professionalism, and we can see their interpersonal skills with others. Those are tangibly observable factors. Often, we are attracted to the visible and perceptible skill sets we see executed by people, and we choose to pursue them for our organizations. We convince ourselves they are a natural and good fit for our organizations. The problem is that data is only surface level.

In order to see what people are really made of, we have to look beyond the surface. We have to get to know people's stories.

So, a good leader must look for the not-so-obvious, the less perceptible, the deeper things to find the real diamonds in the rough. When we look at a person "as is," we are often captivated by irrelevant or distracting data points. As humans, we are attracted to good-looking people. We like people with charisma and drive. We gravitate towards people with positional power, or who are more relationally connected than ourselves. None of those qualities inherently tell us they are a good person, a qualified employee, or someone we'd like to hang out with outside of work hours. In order to see what people are really made of, we have to look beyond the surface. We have to get to know people's stories. We need to see them in action in a number of situations to see how they speak and how they behave. How might they respond to certain pressures over others? When we ask better questions, actually listen, and tease out more specifics, that is when we gain a clearer picture of what we might be working with.

To survey is to examine and record an area and the features of that area. When surveying land for natural resources, like looking for diamonds, one might commission studies and maintain disciplined capital allocation before the commencement of exploration/mining operations for resources. A surveyor may have good instincts, but they don't start petitioning for permits or bringing in crews to dig until the studies verify the deposit. There are actual diamonds out there to discover, and there is inherent value in each one of them, but a survey proves the point. There is an ideology to it all. An experienced surveyor knows that they must actively look into areas that others may altogether overlook. They generally have a different mindset, a different viewpoint, and a different scorecard which they use to qualify where and what they survey. Furthermore, when they uncover the latent gems, they understand that discovery is simply the beginning of a much longer process to fully form and unveil the maximum reflective potential of that diamond. As it relates to human capital, the goal is for a leader to survey those places and spaces where there might be untapped and/ or underutilized individuals, both inside and outside of the existing organization. Additionally, a good surveyor will assess an organization prior to engagement (i.e., risk/reward analysis), and determine if there is sufficient human capital and diversity of gifts already deposited or if they need to go diamond mining. With their expertise, they know what they have and do not have to work with. When they go surveying, they know what they are actually looking for to fill in the gaps and make the best team for the organization. While some leaders are looking all over the place for the "next best employee," the prodigious surveyor will begin with the human capital in their own front yard, with the vision to discover and develop those diamonds in the best manner possible; stewarding them until they reach or at least envision their highest potential.

It is typical of human nature to evaluate people at the surface level. In the positions we find ourselves leading, we all risk making snap judgments and game-time decisions based on what we can readily observe, what we can make sense of, what we can control, and then we filter our analysis through our historical personal experiences. It's a natural way of calculating risk in our decision-making process. The real problem with it all is that we generally face these critical decisions while under the pressure cookers of limited time and limited finances, which can make us impulsive at best and self-sabotaging at worst.

The fact is, as leaders, we don't always get every detail by a cursory glance. There are intangibles that are not overt or obvious. Many of us are guilty of ignoring the volume of human capital right in front of us and the unique value add that each of them would bring to our organizations. The business and other employees end up suffering the consequences of our haste and neglect. When leaders survey for potential human capital, if they don't see the skill set they value most or estimate to be most suited to the job, or if they don't see enough development in their human capital, it's hard for them to move to any sort of action. Even worse, sometimes they actually do see all of the human talent and a modicum of potential, but they are simply too scared to take the chance or put in the work required to get maximum productivity from them. They want the hard work done on their behalf. They want the path of least resistance.

Fundamentally, people believe that skills are either deposited into us from a greater power outside of ourselves and/or were taught and trained in the early formative years of the workforce. This concept is the age-old "nature vs. nurture" conversation. I believe people have already been deposited into at some basic level, and they're just waiting for themselves and their potential to be discovered and developed—given a chance to shine. Since I believe there is inherent worth and value in each individual, it is incumbent upon me to demonstrate that by how I speak of, search for, and support the human capital in my purview.

In fairness, many leaders are ill-equipped to discern the full potential of the human capital around them because they themselves never truly mined nor developed any diamonds—they stole their diamonds from those who mine and actually develop them, leaving myopia, missteps, and/or mismanagement—the perpetual endgame in their leadership and organization. Although a leader might find a diamond with a particular skill that they hold in high regard, that diamond may be a poor fit in so many other areas of the organization that leaving it there not only hurts the company and the team but diminishes the value of the diamond itself.

LOOK FOR SOMETHING SPECIFIC: CULTURAL FIT

One can really get into the weeds when trying to pin down an all-encompassing definition of 'culture,' so for the sake of time, I won't do that. According to Dr. Sam Chand, culture is simply defined as "How we do things here." It's important to know your organizational identity and culture before you go surveying for diamonds because the wrong cultural fit will dilute, distract, delay, or completely destroy how you are doing things. It could also result in killing current team morale, momentum, and maximum productivity.

When you are surveying for diamonds amongst your human capital, you need to first understand a few important principles about their individual culture, because they bring themselves with them to the organization.

1) Pre-Existing Culture

Everyone has a pre-existing culture. How do they view the world? How do they view the workplace and their role in it? How do they plan to live out their life: taking, giving, or some combination of both? Why are they motivated to do any of those things to begin with? The answer to these questions reveals one's pre-existing culture. Generally speaking, family, faith, finances, and geographic environment are early determinants in forming early culture in an individual.

As a surveyor, depending on how close these diamonds may be to your own pre-existing culture (i.e., commonality) or how malleable they are to conform to your viewpoints, the easier you may believe it will be to work with them or assimilate them into your organization. Sometimes the proximity of a shared pre-existing culture works, and sometimes you just get group-think. You end up with organizational toxicity because of the lack of diversity and the ensuing culture clash.

2) Present Culture

This is how things are being done in an organization right now—in real-time. Do you know why you do what you do? Do you know why your team does what they do? Do you like what you see or desire change? If you want change, do you teach, rein-force, and finance for that change or simply demand results with no resources? For better or for worse, culture is dynamic, and it is measurable. So, if you are moving in a particular direction, not only is that observable but the method by which you march in that direction is also telling. People will trust and follow you or they will move on, based on your credibility and trustworthiness according to their pre-existing culture and assessment of your leadership aptitude.

When surveying for diamonds, you need to assess where you are at and where you are going as an organization because a new diamond may be catalytic or cataclysmic to your efforts.

3) Aspirational Culture

This is about future casting and forward momentum. This is all about how you may desire to change the HOW and WHY you presently do things in your organization. Saying you want change versus the action/activity of change are two different things. The changes have to make sense, or you'll end up causing more confusion than good. As a leader, you need to have a clear sense of what you're doing and why. You need to know where you are going and what resources you need to get there. If you have a clarity of culture, you will be able to know who may or may not be a good team fit. You'll know which diamonds to mine for.

Culture trumps vision. It eats strategy for breakfast, but it's shaped and carried out by people.

In his book *Good to Great*, the famed Jim Collins said, "If we get the right people on the bus, the right people in the right seats, and the wrong people off the bus, then we'll figure out how to take it someplace great."[1] This is a matter of cultural fit. Culture trumps vision. It eats strategy for breakfast, but it's shaped and carried out by people. We know that human capital is our most important asset to get things done and get things done THE WAY we want. The collective human capital in an organization shapes, defines, and colors the organizational culture. So, if we take the time and do the hard work to look beyond the surface when surveying human capital in our own front yard but ignore the cultural dynamics that those new diamonds may introduce to our organization, we risk violating our existing culture at the expense of some belief in an aspirational culture, and the result will be frustration at best or complete fracture at worst.

FIVE CRUCIBLES OF CULTURAL FIT

When you go into a jewelry store to look at diamonds, they always look fantastic. The reason they look amazing is because it's all about the lighting they are displayed in. The jewelry case lighting is designed to bring out the proper color and sparkle of each diamond. Light sourcing is specifically made according to a Color Rendering Index (CRI) which tells us the quality of light. The CRI measures the effect a light source has on the perceived color of objects and surfaces. We already know that not every

---

1   Jim Collins, *Good to Great: Why Some Companies Make the Leap and Others Don't* (New York, NY: HarperBusiness, 2001), 42.

diamond in the jewelry case is of the same cut, color, or grade. Yet in different degrees of lighting, they all look enticing. In order not to be deceived, but rather get an honest assessment, it requires the trained eye of a professional jeweler or gemologist with the right tool (a jeweler's loupe) to see past the obvious shine and magnify the minuscule features of each diamond.

We don't have loupes, per se, to help us see every wound, nor every area needing improvement, within our human capital. What we do have are crucibles to flesh those out. Merriam-Webster defines a crucible as "a place or situation in which concentrated forces interact to cause influence, change or development." Crucibles burn chaff and create enough adversity to strengthen and fortify whatever is placed in them. When surveying our pool of diamonds or when we may be looking for new diamonds, it's important to keep these crucibles in mind because they will provide a good litmus test of where the diamonds are and how much further they may need to go in personal development for healthy assimilation into your organization's culture.

Crucible #1: Call

One's calling is a conviction that drives their "yes" and their "no."

If that diamond is called in a particular direction, to a particular vocation, etc., there will be things they just naturally gravitate towards and sacrifices they'll be willing to make. They will model a bias towards action, and it will make sense. It can appear effortless because of the natural inclination within them.

This is observable. Furthermore, leaders must look for a level of self-awareness in them. When diamonds say "yes" to something, they are simultaneously saying "no" to other things. If there is any clarity lacking in one's calling, you'll see conviction vacillate. This fact will be demonstrated by a diamond saying "yes" to things that quite possibly should have been "no" because they actually are not as personally beneficial, nor organizationally effective, as they would like you to believe, but rather serve as a distraction or life detour. No matter how much they try to convince you or themselves, you will see the incongruence play out. You as a leader can gauge the clarity of the diamond via this crucible. Do they know their call?

Crucible #2: Character

One's character is demonstrated in consistent integrity in public and private regardless of the circumstances.

It is largely formed in the trials of life. There are no shortcuts to developing it. You either develop character or you don't. You simply lack it altogether. Character will invariably be in some state of growth and maturation, but it will always be substantive, credible, and dependable. There is no faking it. Cubic zirconia has its place in costume and/or affordable jewelry, but it is a poor substitute for the real thing. You see a diamond is formed under pressure while a cubic zirconia gem is formed in a lab. A diamond is much harder (tougher) in nature, while a cubic zirconia gem is soft. Diamond facets are those small, flat, and polished surfaces located on the crown and the pavilion of the diamond.

A diamond has individual angles of facets that contribute to its uniqueness. A cubic zirconia has soft round edges that give off red, yellow, and blue refraction.

Lack of character is so detrimental to the life of a diamond and to your organization that a surveyor cannot afford to ignore it. This crucible will expose the occlusions and impurities in a diamond. While it may not be a deal breaker, it will give a surveyor the most accurate picture of what they are working with.

Crucible #3: Competency

One's competency is their ability to do something and do it to a desired standard.

Certain jobs require levels of specific competency that are not necessarily required of other jobs. Regardless of the simple or complex nature of the jobs in your organization, there is still a level of competency needed to get the job done in a manner that accurately conveys the culture espoused by you as a leader. Knowing the necessary competencies required to promote someone out of their current role is just as important as knowing the required competencies to do a job in the first place because you can promote someone right out of their best contribution. This crucible is very important.

Crucible #4: Capacity

One's capacity is the margin/bandwidth to demonstrate their present competencies and grow new ones. Capacity is more multifaceted and dynamic than most people give it credit for. There is physical capacity, emotional capacity, resource capacity, and organizational capacity that either act as a floor or ceiling for the diamond. Capacity can be grown. The levels of capacity within a diamond in each of those areas will give the surveyor a wider and deeper insight into actual yield.

Crucible #5: Chemistry

Chemistry is a measure of likability and fit within a specific culture.

We spend a lot of time at work, so it is really nice to work with people you actually like. If someone has competency but they aren't much fun to be around, you should think long and hard about those diamonds staying in your setting. The soft skills to get along with others and to model your organization's aspirational culture hinge upon this crucible. Let it tell you the truth about a person and about a situation. Do not dismiss this. A word of caution: don't mix up character and chemistry. Some diamonds may have plenty of character and simply not be a good fit in your culture.

LOOK FOR WHAT IS IN THE BEST INTEREST OF THE DIAMOND

An orange seed will never produce an apple tree, no matter how frequently you water it, fertilize it, or pray over it. Neither can an apple seed grow into an orange tree. In fact, if you studied the two fruits, you would understand that they need very different conditions to thrive.

*A good leader will not hoard nor hold
back a diamond from their best setting.*

An apple seed grows an apple tree which then produces apples. In order for that apple tree to bear good apples, it must endure a tough winter. The resilience that is cultivated from that adversity results in a better harvest.

An orange seed grows an orange tree which then produces oranges. However, an orange tree actually cannot handle even the mildest of winters. Too much cold, frost, and adversity will not fortify the tree but will kill it and make it non-fruit bearing—not only for that season but potentially for all future seasons.

While I believe that we need to look beyond the surface and look for specific cultural fit guided by the five crucibles, I acknowledge that not everyone thrives in the same environment. A good leader will not hoard nor hold back a diamond from their best setting. A good leader will behave in a manner that considers what is in the best interest of the diamond. If a leader helps the diamond find its best setting, that leader may feel shy of a diamond but will have actually multiplied their influence and scope as well as fortified their loyalty and trust—by acting in the best interest of the diamond at the perceived detriment of the organization. It may seem counterintuitive, but real trust is formed when you put others before yourself.

CHAPTER 2

EXCAVATING
CLEAR THE PAIN

W hen I was developing land in Washington State, I bought a piece of land overlooking the Columbia River Gorge. It was one of, if not the first, homes built on the hillside. It had the original well that supplied water to nineteen or so homes that were eventually built in the neighborhood. On my property was an upper, middle, and lower flag lot. The middle lot had a barn and a three-storied house with an unobstructed view of the Columbia River and Mt. Hood in the distance on the Oregon side. Adjacent to the upper lot, cascading side by side at a 45-degree downward slope just behind the barn, were three newer homes. Adjacent to the lower flag lot to the side of the barn was another random neighbor. This was the lowest-situated home before there was my wide-open field in the lower flag lot.

In the Pacific Northwest, water is supplied in abundance from the ground and the sky. One particularly rainy day, the neighbor who lived in the lowest situated home, next to the barn, came to my door and started yelling at my wife. It was shocking because we didn't have a deep relationship and he didn't come to have a civil conversation. He just came, hot and heavy, verbally assaulting my wife. He was complaining to her about his garage flooding and demanded we fix it before he reported us to the city and sued us for damages. When I came home from work, my wife asked me to look into it. All I could see was that there was natural water runoff. Living on a granite hillside below five other homes, you are going to see some water runoff. I reached out to the city, and they concurred with my assessment. That was simply the result of where he built his house. I'm not sure what the original city planner was thinking allowing that in the first place. Possibly the city wanted more income, so they let people build whatever, wherever, they wanted. All I know is that everything was laid out and city-approved before I bought the property, so I wasn't going to take responsibility for nature's gift, however unfortunate it was for my neighbor.

A few weeks later, we had another particularly wet day, but this time you could really see water gushing out of a dirt bank, pouring right into this guy's garage. Once again, he became verbally belligerent to my wife while I was at work. I came home and assessed the situation. I decided to try and help, even though this was natural water runoff. I began to trench out some areas to see if there were any busted water drains, or anything possibly not on old blueprints. I didn't find anything, so I trenched a line to channel the water runoff into my field. I didn't know how else to help. It didn't really work and now the neighbor was complaining I manufactured runoff onto his property. Once again, the city came out and I explained my attempt to aid him, but at the end of the day, I didn't build my house that low and this is the result of nature. While the city agreed with me, I didn't want the neighbor to continue badgering my wife while I worked. I was at a loss for how to fix this situation.

That is when one of the other neighbors came to our rescue. She decided to buy the man's house from him. The day escrow closed, she sawed down six trees and then came to speak with me. In order to preserve her newest acquisition, she paid to have a French drain put in on my side of the fence, running down into my field. I asked her why she would spend that kind of money and pay for something that wasn't necessarily her responsibility. She told me, "That neighbor has consistently been a pain in my rear over the years. He intentionally planted those trees to block my river view, and I don't like how he's treating your wife! I got the money, so I made the decision to get him out of here."

Sometimes, we have to clear the pain. In order to clear the pain, however, it incurs costs. In this case, it came at the cost of a second home and a small excavating project, but the neighborhood definitely became more peaceful when that obstacle was removed.

After you and I survey the land and determine that it has valuables hidden throughout the estate, we have to deal with some costs. There are up-front costs in purchasing property. There are taxes being accrued on that property. There are permitting fees at the stage you want to alter that land in any way. In order to excavate and get to the diamonds that are buried in that ground, we have to start with the permitting.

PERMITTING

Permitting is all about permission. When we as surveyors turn to excavators and plan to encroach upon someone's life and upend it in many ways, knowing it will be messy and painful, we have to get permission first. If there is no permission given, there is no way that excavation can begin. Diamonds ultimately have to want to be found, dug up, and developed. They have to consent to the season(s) of discomfort and unearthing. When a diamond invites us to assist them, despite the ensuing difficulties ahead, they cannot blame, accuse, or play the victim in any manner. They chose to bring in the necessary help to get them to their desired destination. Permission is the initial investment needed to deal with later collateral damage that may come in the process because it will be rough.

Another word I like to use is "agreement." Permission is allowing one to move forward with something, but to me, agreement includes a level of clarity and understanding, not simply consent. Like when you go to the doctor and you sign paperwork, you are giving permission for the staff to look up health records, run your insurance, and perform any required medical services. Yet every doctor knows that when it comes time to give a shot or do anything that may cause pain or emotional duress, they need to use their bedside manner and explain how things are going to transpire to the best of their ability. They should seek for their patient to understand to the fullest possible degree and agree to it, knowing full well how uncomfortable and/or unsuccessful the care provided may be. Agreement involves clear expectations and some personal ownership in the process. Again, no victim mentality here.

On the other hand, when a doctor knows you are coming to them as a professional, extending a level of trust and implied permission for them to examine and possibly diagnose but then they don't communicate, don't listen, and resent you giving any input at all, you find an impasse—a lack of agreement. Any further movement on the part of the physician would actually be a violation.

When excavation is necessary, cities charge permitting fees and impose taxes or seek bond measures to give themselves a pool of money to better care for the city and to handle contingencies. When citizens vote for how to best use that money, they can choose between parks and recreation services, road repairs, better police and fire services, etc. There are many areas that may need improvement in the city, but there are always limited cash supplies. Likewise, when we plan to excavate in people's lives, there may be many areas that when exposed need shoring up. However, we must choose which areas to prioritize with specificity and intentionality and get agreement so we can use our resources wisely.

To that point, permits outline the specific parameters of what you are allowed to do and what you are forbidden to do lest you get fined or shut down entirely. It is not only okay, but it is essential, to continuously outline the parameters of the excavation process.

Lastly, permits are not indefinite. They are for a specified season to accomplish a specific goal. If one cannot do the work in the agreed-upon time frame, there is an expectation to pull new permits and get more agreement. That rest often comes with additional cost as well.

DIGGING

Excavation is hard work. You have to show up at the work site before the sun rises. The day generally starts out cold and dark, but by first light, everyone has worked up a sweat and you start peeling layers. If it's a sunny day, you know it's going to be a long day because you are trying to dig through dirt that doesn't want to give. If it's a rainy day, you know it's going to be long because although you can dig more easily, the ground can also erode and backfill what you just trenched. It might even be too soggy to get the necessary machinery positioned to do the required work. It is dangerous because of the machinery, the weather conditions, and because the earth you are moving can actually bury you alive. Sometimes the danger isn't even from the tools or ground itself, but circumstances around the job site that are out of your control. For instance, road construction workers occasionally lose their lives due to a poor driver who veers into a work site.

When we are dealing with our human capital, the actual people we are excavating are going to be in a sunny disposition some days, and other days, not so much. Understand the climate before you begin. Sometimes they'll be malleable and other times pretty calloused. Sometimes the distraction or deterrent is completely outside of the excavation process, but it inserts itself nonetheless. Either way, excavation will be hard work.

You will find that in order to get access to those diamonds, you will have to get through a lot of obstacles, and many of those obstacles are painful.

To do excavation properly, you have to get all your safety gear on, which generally consists of a hard hat, steel-toed boots, a neon yellow shirt, a reflective vest, some eye goggles, ear plugs, and tough gloves for hand protection. Some of the group drives machinery while others are standing all day, using hand tools to get where the machines cannot reach. There are real obstacles around the excavation of diamonds. If one believes the diamonds are there and deserve to be seen in their best light, one must be willing to use all the tools at their disposal to overcome any obstacle and unearth those diamonds. Sometimes this involves basic hand tools and other times it takes heavy machinery. Most of the time it requires both. Make sure you have the full tool set in place for the whole job, not just a task. Possibly make sure you have a team ready to cover areas you alone cannot get to.

Once you have surveyed the land, determined there are diamonds to unearth, counted the cost, and pulled permits, it's time to start digging. You will likely have seen some surface-level impediments like tree stumps or trash heaps, but when you start digging, you often come up against large boulders, the tree stumps' sprawling root systems, and other rubble that is keeping latent talent buried beneath them. You will find that in order to get access to those diamonds, you will have to get through a lot of obstacles, and many of those obstacles are painful. Painful for you and for the diamond.

For example, I have been teaching leadership development and giving young people early access to opportunities not usually afforded them. Oftentimes I will use the opportunities to work alongside them and flesh out specific blind spots, immaturities, or character flaws that are obvious and observable hindrances to those individuals. At times, those shortcomings could be worked through pretty easily. The hard part was whenever I dug into a pain point and found that those young people's pre-existing culture, their lack of self-awareness, and their addiction to pleasing people (i.e., especially their parents) were hindering their ability to address those blind spots, immaturities, and character flaws. The very source of those observable issues was actually deeper and more entangled than what anyone could have seen on the surface. In those situations, one cannot simply stop trying to address the bad fruit by plucking and discarding that fruit. You have to get to the root of the situation. All of a sudden you will find yourself poking into areas that you didn't get "agreement" from yet are necessary obstacles to remove for the sake of that individual—and things just get really uncomfortable.

What obstacles keep us—the excavator—from seeing or getting to the diamonds right in front of us? It could have originally been our ignorance of the diamonds within our organization or our resistant ideology to the diamond mining process altogether. It could be our current lack of good systems and structures to care for the diamonds we might unearth. Meaning that we may not have the present capacity to handle the onboarding or be equipped to give clear directions for such an influx. It might be our lack of budget, our poor recruiting messaging, a non-existent pipeline, a limited network, etc. Maybe the obstacles are a bit more entangled and not simply organizational shortfalls alone. Possibly the diamond is underqualified at present or the timing to hire/promote isn't in sync with the organization. Sometimes there is a lack of availability.

A common frustration I hear from business owners and company managers is that they feel they are having to parent children instead of managing adult employees. They lament providing income while their human capital isn't quite at a desired maturity level. They cite the different work ethics, different skill sets, and in many cases, some stunted emotional intelligence in the current generation flooding into the marketplace.

To some degree, this is how every preceding working group feels about each subsequent wave of future human capital. There is a feeling of "I had to pay my dues, I had to acquiesce to a particular work climate, whether I liked it or not, so I expect others after me will do the same."

Each wave that enters the workforce comes with its pre-existing cultures and they fight to assimilate into the current culture (self-preservation) with hopes that they might be a contributor to the aspirational culture of the organization.

There are pros and cons, both in culture and skill set, to the contributions that each group has brought to the marketplace. So, if the current wave of workers needs some attention and coaching in areas you and I take for granted, we have to be willing to go there. The benefit is they may have something to teach us, too.

When we really dig past the generational work differences, we see that all people in our organizations—the diamonds in the rough—need to be set free, unlocked, untangled, unencumbered, etc. They need sponsorship and advocacy whether they know it or not. In order for our human capital to become who they were always designed to be, we as leaders need to meet them where they are, walk alongside them, remove unnecessary obstacles for them, make opportunities for them, and remain consistent and present throughout. This is largely about earning trust and freeing them up to work on other areas in their lives.

DISCERNINGLY DETANGLE

There is a heavy cost to this excavation process, as you can only dig as far as there is agreement, and like most manual work, the job you see on the surface is rarely the entirety of the job you will have to execute. Hence the need for change orders and/or renegotiation of terms lest you bite off more than you can chew and end up eating up your profit with all of the extra costs involved. While not everyone will willingly submit to the discomforts involved, many will. Getting initial permission and/or agreement is actually the easiest part because you believe you know who you are working with and somewhat of a scope of the work involved. The harder part is when you come across things, areas, or circumstances that you didn't originally know would be involved with the job. No expressed permission or agreement knew the level of entanglement you were about to uncover. Outside of the certain levels or degrees of agreement, as one digs through layer after layer, scraping back the dirt until you'll get a clearer view of the entire picture that you are working with, only then can you begin to make informed assessments about which obstacles are truly hurting and which obstacles are actually helping that diamond. At first glance, it can look like a simple job. As you dig, you begin to see more details, complexities, and entanglements. A wise excavator always reserves a level of discernment on the timing and totality of an excavation job because there are inevitable surprises with every job and every diamond. Things just aren't always as they appear.

For example, some tree stumps and boulders are weighing a diamond down, crushing them under their weight. As that relates to human capital, let's call those tree stumps and boulders inferiority, insecurity, ineptitude, and other lies. However, some obstacles are helpful and serve as a way of preventing natural erosion that could wash our diamonds away entirely. As that relates to human capital, let's call those boundaries expectations, deadlines, and cautions. Sometimes when our human capital has spent a significant amount of time buried, they themselves cannot tell which obstacles are attacking them or aiding them. So a leader, an excavator, needs to think through the bigger picture. Instead of hastily tossing dirt and potentially taking out some underground fiber optics line or other utilities (i.e., digging up a historical family wound), a careful excavator will know how to grade dirt and maneuver those potentially emotional pain points.

If you want to get the most out of your diamonds, you may have to dig deeper and wider than you originally may have thought.

When you dig through the major obstacles surrounding a person's life, it can be exhausting, and it often takes more of your energy and willpower than you most likely originally estimated. Without a proper and fuller perspective, it can be pretty discouraging when you dig up a diamond and they aren't all shiny and pretty. In fact, they are often raw, undeveloped, and surrounded by some level of self-protective rock layer. They are crusty. People have very real physical, emotional, spiritual, and cultural barriers to their own development. Sometimes organizations may inadvertently be designed in such a way that they create unnecessary growth barriers/ceilings for their human capital. If you want to get the most out of your diamonds, you may have to dig deeper and wider than you originally may have thought. You will have to be discerning when to bring out the heavy equipment and when you will have to move beyond it and transition into more delicate and precise tools that help shape the actual diamond itself.

CHAPTER 3

SHAPING

MEAN WHAT YOU SAY

The state of Oregon is known for multiple mountain ranges, pristine lakes, high deserts, open prairies, lush farmlands, and incredibly dense forests that stretch north and south, border to border, chock-full of one hundred-foot-tall evergreen trees reaching up to the gray skies overhead. It is a nature lover's paradise.

While many of my peers enjoyed the snow-capped bodies of Mt. Hood or Mt. Bachelor, I preferred to spend my time at the Oregon coast. If you are from the Pacific Northwest, you understand that there is a clear difference between a beach and a coast. First off, if you're landlocked, you may call a riverbank or lakeside "the beach," but you'd be wrong. To any sane person, a beach makes one think of sunny days, surfing waves, warm water, making sandcastles, playing frisbee, and eventually eating some good seafood. If you were looking for a beach in Oregon, you'd be wrong too. Oregon has a coastline.

The Oregon coast is overcast with beady horizontal rainfall that beats down on you mercilessly. It is endlessly windy and cold, only occasionally clearing up when you least expect it. Despite the conditions, kite flying is a fan favorite. The grassy hills on the coastal cliffs look down on long stretches of sand dunes that are great for racing dune buggies. The sand hills taper off into flat shorelines that are littered with boulders and driftwood. Seashells and seaweed are exposed each morning as the saltwater tides flow to the sea, leaving nothing but a blanket of yellow seafoam in its wake. The Oregon coast has its own beauty, for sure, but I would not call it "a beach."

There are plenty of jetties to fish off of and whales to watch for, but watersport is not a premium on the Oregon coast. Sure, you can roll up your pant legs and freeze your toes, but if you like surfing, you need an 8mm wetsuit with a hoodie. The Pacific Ocean has a cold-water current known as the "California Current" and it travels south from British Columbia, Canada, following the US coastline all the way down to Mexico. Oregon sits in the middle of that pathway and the water is literally body-numbing cold. For those of us who were crazy enough to play in the Oregon coastal waters, there were some basic lessons you adhered to. Only go out to your waist so you keep a good footing. Secondly, only stay in long enough to avoid hypothermia. Lastly, and most importantly, keep looking back at the shore to make sure the riptides and undertow don't pull you out to sea. The oceanic floor drastically drops off less than a football field's length out into the ocean, so while wave hopping is a frequent dare of choice, it's not all that recreational. At least not in the daytime.

The true secret to playing in the Oregon coastal waters is to go in the midnight hours. After the sun has heated up the sand all day and the waves have churned that sand up, the thermocline is significantly warmer than in the daytime. That is why my friends and I, living inland just thirty to forty minutes away, would make midnight runs to the coast.

His plea sent shivers up and down my spine. He started yelling that he couldn't touch the seafloor anymore.

On one such occasion, as seniors in high school, we went to Newport, Oregon, for a shoreline run. On that particular evening, the moon lit up the water just enough for us to cast aside all fear of Jaws eating us for a midnight snack, and we decided we wanted to jump "warmer" ocean waves. One doesn't really jump the waves, we just bounce off the seafloor like pogo sticks, trying to make sure the waves never crest our heads but only splash our chests. Being of varied heights, this was easier said than done. My friends all stood over six feet, and I at a generous 5' 3". We all pogoed in different spots so as not to get in over our heads. The water was warm, but it was still a bit eerie. On this occasion, my best friend since second grade was catching waves just a touch farther out than me when he screamed for me. It took me by surprise because everything had been fun and the water was relatively calm, but being friends that long, I knew he was serious. His plea sent shivers up and down my spine. He started yelling that he couldn't touch the seafloor anymore. The seafloor must have washed out a little closer to the shoreline than we anticipated, and he was rightfully terrified. In that moment I had to decide to go past where I could touch to help him or let him drown. I opted for the prior. As I swam toward him, I kept yelling, "Ray, I'm coming. I will not leave you behind. Ray, I'll swim to you. Relax, tread water, and breathe." I wasn't sure at what point the tide was pulling out too strong or if I could even get Ray calm enough to swim with me, but I had to try. I had heard horror stories that lifeguards occasionally had to straight up punch a person and/or knock them out to keep them from panicking and pulling the both of them to the ocean depths. Fortunately, Ray trusted me at my word, so when I made it to him and put my arm around him, he didn't flail. I asked him to help me kick towards the shore and he did. Eventually, we got in far enough where he could touch the ground again. From there he bounced and pulled me back to a manageable depth.

For years Ray and I had known each other. We played sports, had sleepovers, got into trouble, and had maybe one real fight. We knew each other's strengths and weaknesses, but what mattered in that moment wasn't the dirt we had on each other; it was the trust that we had built. We were friends who kept our word. Our word was our bond. So, when I told Ray I wouldn't leave him to drown in the Pacific Ocean, he knew I meant what I said, no matter how improbable it felt at that moment.

The phrase "My word is my bond" can be traced back in English literature to Shakespeare's time and is referred to in the Merchant of Venice.[2] In 1670, the phrase appears in John

---

2   William Shakespeare, "The Merchant of Venice," play.

Ray's English proverbs like this: "An honest man's word is as good as his bond." "My word is my bond" is also the motto of the London Stock Exchange (LSE). The motto is believed to express and encourage adherence to the highest standards of integrity in financial markets. Its origins include its use to create binding agreements without the need for written forms of contract. This is about trust.

Stephen M. R. Covey explains in his book, *The Speed of Trust,* that trust is the great liberator of time and resources and an essential condition for growth. He argues that "When trust goes up, speed will also go up and cost will go down," and that "When trust goes down, speed will go down and costs will go up."[3] Covey explains that the speed at which you can grow your business is directly proportional to the time that you invest in creating trusting relationships.

What does a trusting relationship look like? This can be expressed by its antithesis. When you can't be taken at your word, you have nothing—no trust and no followership. Anyone of us can say anything we want, at any moment, for any particular reason, to drive towards a desired outcome. We may be afraid. We may be political. We may even be manipulative. If we are short-sighted and lead from those places, we will not garner the buy-in we actually desire. People will see our actions and determine the sincerity of our speech. They will critique our

---

3   Steven Covey, *The Speed of Trust: The One Thing That Changes Everything* (New York, NY: Free Press, 2008).

words and our deeds, both in private and in public, measuring our consistency and faithfulness.

Our diamonds, even when we have unearthed them and cleared whatever is cluttering their lives, will most likely still have a tough exterior and a self-protective posture. In order to do the necessary shaping of that diamond, they have to trust you. You and I earn trust when we "say what we mean and mean what we say," letting our actions mirror what we espouse.

Excavation is demonstrated by counting the cost, setting expectations upfront, and having real agreement. Trust begins to be accrued when the diamonds are no longer physically trapped, forcing them to behave or respond in an unnatural or unhealthy manner. When an excavator gets a diamond into a healthy environment to continue the deeper work still ahead and the diamond isn't feeling controlled, manipulated, or any unhealthy pressure, only then can trust truly form.

Ultimately, we can teach what we know but we will reproduce who we are.

As trust is beginning and is in its most basic and tenuous state, we test those waters when we turn to the diamond cutter who actually shapes the diamond. A diamond cutter breaks off the crusty exterior, chips away at the rough edges, buffs out the occlusions, and cuts the diamond into a specific shape so that it can actually reveal what it was designed to reflect. The diamond cutter knows this must be done with extreme precision and is often a progressive process, beginning as agonizingly painful and moving towards step-by-step healing. In order to maintain trust throughout the process, the diamond shaper has to be upfront about the pain and they must proceed with caution and care, frequently revisiting that original agreement, to make sure the end goal is still shared. Like a dentist watching every flinch or tensing of their patient's body while drilling out a cavity and adjusting accordingly to maintain trust in the cutting process, one must demonstrate the wisdom to have frequent communication and some healthy accountability to ensure that even in the pain of it all, the actions being taken are, first and foremost, beneficial for your human capital. If it's good for the diamond, in the overall scope of things it will be good for the organization. Without this constant calibration, a diamond can lose trust and choose to tap out from this developmental journey, even if it is premature and to his or her own detriment.

Ultimately, we can teach what we know but we will reproduce who we are. So while we want to pour into others, we have to be aware of what we are pouring into ourselves first. What we consume affects how we believe and how we shape those diamonds. It will overflow into the projects we touch and the diamonds whose lives we speak into. If we want to be leaders of organizational cultures who are trustworthy and truly in the business of diamond mining, we as leaders cannot escape our own personal development, because we need to have new things to share with our diamonds. If we circumvent the shaping stage within ourselves, our existing human capital will pay the price. To miss this fact is to lose trust in our human capital from the onset. This is the old adage, "Don't ask somebody to do anything you wouldn't be willing to do yourself." So, we don't posture ourselves in a manner that is superior or removed from teaching. Rather, we model for others what it looks like to care well for oneself and remain a continual learner.

When leaders devalue both personal development and the development of others, they will eventually and needlessly lose the diamonds right in their care.

Some leaders and organizations don't take the advice they so frequently peddle to others, demonstrated by poor physical health, deteriorating family dynamics, and a lack of engagement in basic civic and community activities. They don't do enough continuing education. They don't take appropriate vacation time. They often mix up their priorities, emphasizing work over family. They don't know their neighbors. When these leaders and/or organizations lack a healthy routine of self-care and per-sonal investment, it's no wonder we don't see diamonds being shaped the way that they should be. At a core level, these leaders don't value development in general, so it's no surprise they aren't even noticing the diamonds in front of them, let alone thinking about developing them. When leaders devalue both personal development and the development of others, they will eventually and needlessly lose the diamonds right in their care.

A common tendency for a leader who doesn't recognize the talent under their nose will be to jump to outsourcing or importing talent when there is an organizational vacancy. When an organization headhunts talent from another organization, they are often chasing after a skillset alone. That talent might have an admirable skillset but may also lack the proper cultural fit with the pursuing organization. I call this behavior "stealing diamonds," and the perpetrator a "diamond thief." The issue isn't that there may ever be a legitimate situation where your organization needs outside help. The issue is that most solutions can be solved with existing internal human capital and may not require outside help to begin with. A leader may not know the fullness of their existing pool of talent, and to headhunt or "steal diamonds" not only risks dilution of the organizational culture, but it risks simultaneously robbing potential growth opportunities from the existing human capital. For your human capital, this sort of behavior erodes trust in the organization as well as confidence in themselves. So, a good leader will keep a pulse on their diamonds and what stage of development may be needed. Again, I contrast the thief and miner to demonstrate the degree to which an organization will work with what they've got, work through the issues that arise, and work together towards an aspirational goal versus looking for that silver bullet employee outside of the cultural "circle of trust."

My experience over the years has shown me that leaders have limitations to the volume of people they can pour into, the nature and scope of what they can cover, and the length of time they can sustain their efforts. This is perfectly natural. My problem is that they either don't value development entirely and/or they lack the clarity behind their actions. Some organizations work with people but to a limited degree, yet they try to pass it off as more than it actually is. They may do philanthropic deeds together, like feeding the homeless or serving on an overseas mission trip. They might identify an "up-and-comer" and opt to have a good conversation while sharing a meal together. They do these activities and then tell themselves that they are automatically developing their human capital. In truth, they are simply doing some good deeds, hanging out, and sharing a meal. These actions aren't inherently bad; they aren't necessarily great either. Without a level of intentionality, getting to those conversations where you ask hard questions, and pull back those painful layers that will eventually lead to deep, visible, and lasting change is next to impossible. There has to be some frequency involved too. Unfortunately, I have witnessed a continual inability or reluctance in the market from various organizations to do actual diamond mining. They appear to be doing external tactics that look like they are shaping a diamond, but in reality, they're lacking intentionality and unveil/expose themselves as unfruitful labor. This fails the trust test. Let me explain what I mean. If we want to see our human capital thrive and our diamonds shine, we must understand the different methods of shaping that take place in our world so as not to confuse our actions and/or expectations with our efforts. Furthermore, we should look at the following sequential examples and properly gauge where we are on the sliding fulcrum of trust. With each successive method, I would submit that there is a deeper level of trust gained, and if a diamond wants to reach its maximum clarity, it needs to make it to the final stage.

TEACHER

A teacher is recognized for having information to impart or disseminate to a particular audience. The information feed is solely unidirectional—from teacher to student. The audience size is irrelevant. It can be big, or it can be small. The whole exchange is a matter of transferring knowledge. There is a minimal level of trust afforded a teacher until they satisfy the natural skepticism/suspicions of the student.

Teachers are not inherently mentoring their students, nor are they disciple-making. However, the good teachers, when we reflect back on them, are eventually sought after and seen as mentors. That just isn't the initial conception of the relationship.

MENTOR

A mentor is also recognized for having information to impart or disseminate to a particular audience. The direction of that information is still singularly unidirectional—from expert to learner. The difference here is that mentors are generally seen as subject matter experts (SMEs). Their audience size is typically smaller. The mentee (i.e., student) seeks out the mentor (i.e., teacher) to acquire insight, knowledge, and practical steps on a "specific" topic. While mentoring is a transfer of specific knowledge, it is seasonal learning. The scope (breadth and width) of impartation is varied because many students will come and go after they get the information they seek. Agreement of terms are subject to termination at the discretion of the mentor or mentee at any time. There is a higher degree of trust implied in a mentor/mentee relationship demonstrated by the very fact that the mentee seeks out the mentor, not the other way around. Due to the volume of consumable information and topics to study, it is feasible that one might have multiple mentors in a lifetime. Mentors are not inherently disciple-making, but they will employ some aspect of teaching.

Dr. Morris Dirks claims there is a mentoring continuum, and this is a main source of confusion about what mentorship is, in my view. A continuum is a continuous sequence in which adjacent elements are not perceptibly different from each other, although the extremes are quite distinct. The continuum is Active Mentoring—Occasional Mentoring—Passive Mentoring. You go from "more deliberate" to "less deliberate." Active Mentoring would involve disciple-making, spiritual advising, and coaching. Occasional Mentoring would involve counseling, teaching, sponsoring, and being a boss. Passive Mentoring would be a "contemporary model" (i.e., industry peer or present-day author), a "historical model" (i.e., an inspiring historical character or an ancient author), or a "divine contact" (i.e., where you have seen or read about acts of God).

There are Mentoring Dynamics:

TYPE OF DYNAMIC	NAME OF DYNAMIC
Initiate the Process	Attraction
Major Means	Relationship
Crucial Details of Empowering Relationship	Responsiveness and Accountability

The end result or goal of a healthy mentoring dynamic is "empowerment and trust." Hopefully, this will lead to a disciple-making relationship.

Remember, in order to learn a great many things, you will need to seek out multiple mentors—individuals you can trust. Over a lifetime, that diverse relational network of healthy mentors will be the catalyst for growth in your life and the inspiration to "pay it forward." It is the gateway to the final stage of disciple-making. This is where a diamond gets those finishing touches in the shaping process.

Side note: If you are not yet sure who is discipling you or who you should disciple, or if there is not yet enough trust formed to submit at a true discipleship-making level, it's okay to begin with mentorship. Just understand that with each mentor you learn from, they impart to you their knowledge along with their pre-existing culture. So be discerning and don't let it dilute your aspirational culture in the process.

DISCIPLE-MAKER

Disciple-making is different from teaching and mentoring. Teaching and mentoring both involve the transferring of information: some opinions, some good advice, and hopefully some best practices. Teaching and mentoring both disseminate their information in the singularly one-way direction—the model of expert to learner, usually lecturing to their audience. The audience size varies in teaching and mentoring but typically it is progressively smaller, with mentorship being a handful of seasonal students hungry to gain more insight on a focused topic.

Disciple-making is the most intimate stage of earned trust and it is the ultimate goal in this diamond-shaping process.

In both teaching and mentoring, the student seeks out the learning and can do whatever they choose to with the information they receive. While the information being shared may or may not be immediately applicable to their lives, the information is actually not the main point. This is all a progression of earning trust. Disciple-making is the most intimate stage of earned trust and it is the ultimate goal in this diamond-shaping process.

Disciple-maker is different from teaching and mentoring in the fact that it is a two-way conversation, demonstrated by living life-on-life together. It is less about oratory behavior (i.e., lecturing) to pass along information and more about modeling a way to live in a shared environment.

THE 4 'I'S' OF DISCIPLE-MAKING

Invited

The disciple-maker can sense that there is a level of trust with someone they have taught or mentored up to this point. They can tell when the trust factor has reached the place where they have so much agreement that they can press into the deeper levels for real-life change. The disciple-maker seeks out the disciple, not the other way around. They establish who they want to live life with and they invite them into this relationship. There is a belief that both the disciple-maker and disciple share, that this relationship is the best way forward for all parties involved.

Intimate

The disciple-maker pursues the disciple and agrees to avail themself and their resources to invest in that disciple. There is full transparency on the table and the curtain is pulled back so that the disciple can make sense of how the disciple-maker is living and emulate it. The lessons learned come in sharing life in real-time, with details, and debriefs. The lessons that are learned are acute and precise, often referencing the decision a disciple may choose to make and the thought processes involved. This level of intimacy can only be had when the trust level is high.

Invasive

In order to shape a diamond with the precision necessary to reach his or her ultimate refraction level, the disciple agrees to a level of inquiry, inspection, interpreting, and informing from the disciple-maker. This can be uncomfortable at times. This will most definitely be painful. This insistence to press past the excuses, the insecurities, or any other defense mechanism is the only way to get to true places of perspective, healing, and growth. Just as the disciple-maker agrees to share themselves and their resources, in exchange they ask to go to those internal places that most people just don't allow others into. Of course, the goal isn't to know all the dirt and expose the disciple's vulnerabilities. We always go back to the rule where we put the interest of the diamond above the organization. So, any digging or demolition that transpires is for the benefit of the diamond you are discipling.

Intentional

This particular point cannot be overstated. Aspirational objectives, the methods that will be employed, and the timeline or season to execute these all should be clearly outlined and agreed to. This level of intentionality is so specific that even when you communicate the plan, you need to be ready to explain, revisit, and even pivot along the way. At no time should either party not understand what is going on. If intentionality and trust are paramount, then even when there are lessons for a disciple to learn in an unfamiliar situation, the disciple will know that the disciple-maker will break it down with them. Any experience and/or crucible will not be in vain.

Shaping diamonds is hands-on, messy, and laborious in nature.

So, disciple-makers are not the same as teachers and mentors, but they do teach and mentor. They just go beyond those two levels and model the 4 'I's.' There are faith communities that emphasize teaching from their pulpits on Sundays or some specific classes they have programming around and they call it discipleship, but that is teaching only. Institutions of higher education claim discipleship, but their primary offering is teaching. Some faith communities go a little further and say they focus on mentoring, but that too is debatable. They might have coffee or share a meal with someone, or they might go to a conference, but if they aren't in agreement or focusing on a specific area of growth, it's just a hang-out. Getting volunteers to share in the workload of your weekend service production is just that—volunteerism. It may or may not be a springboard to a deeper and more intentional relationship. Again, if there isn't specificity of training, with hope of life transformation, it isn't mentorship. If one doesn't actually do or move beyond teaching and mentoring, you just don't ever get to real disciple-making. It's impossible to shape a diamond to the degree necessary through simple lectures and sidebar conversations. Shaping diamonds is hands-on, messy, and laborious in nature.

These same examples apply to any organization in the marketplace. Getting thrown into work with no training at all or just being given the company handbook is not equivalent to onboarding. Pitting employees against each other does not lead to collaboration or a posture of teachability where one might risk getting help from a tenured peer. Working a job with no sponsorship, peer-coaching, or protégé program is the exact opposite culture of a diamond-shaping one.

True disciple-making is not scalable, at least not in the obvious first-glance sort of way. It is not about standardization or efficiency. It's one-on-one, tailored to that specific diamond, and works towards the best shaping of that gem. I will say, however, that when multiple people begin to do this right and disciples turn into disciple-makers, then it will appear to be happening at scale. The day-to-day exchange, though, is more intimate and dynamic for this to be some sort of templated, one-size-fits-all process.

After the enormous risk of surveying and the excruciating labor around excavating, one still must ask: "Is it worth the effort to shape what we uncover?" Chipping away the rough areas takes time—and it has to be agreed upon. You don't get agreement if they don't believe you at your word or that the inevitable cutting is in "their best interest." That is a matter of trust. Fundamentally a diamond shaper believes the cutting (pruning/shaping/refining, etc.) is in the best interest of the gem and the diamond agrees. When the right cuts are made, the gem will reflect and refract in a special way, according to the fashion it was designed to do.

CHAPTER 4

SETTING
GIVE IT AWAY

I am a stereotypical Gen Xer—born in 1976 and raised through the 80s and 90s. I was the youngest of four boys from a military household. Due to those specific early life choices, my parents' college careers got started later in life when my brothers and I were in the middle of adolescence. While our parents worked their day jobs and took college classes simultaneously, the four of us were left alone to manage our own days to a large degree. We had the obligatory house chores and errands to do, but our jobs were principally to keep our grades up, stay active, and stay out of trouble. As siblings, we succeeded at staying active.

While our parents were pretty busy, they made sure that we were enrolled in some kind of sports year-round. Thus, I have had a lifelong obsession with sports. Living in the Pacific Northwest meant we played seasonal sports, unlike my peers in the sunny South who might have specialized. I played football, basketball, wrestling, and baseball all the way through my eighth-grade year. My favorite was basketball.

When I began my high school journey, I entered my freshman year at 4' 6", 65 pounds. Yes, I know that is the size of most elementary school children. I know this all too well because when I was a visiting high school band student at a regional Oregon elementary school, the teacher/chaperone mistakenly tried to corral me to class with the kiddos until my classmates came to my rescue. That's a story for another day. I was so short and thin that I couldn't find jeans that fit me. I wore sweatpants, shorts, or dress slacks practically all of my freshman year. When I came to high school, because of my size, there was a lot of pressure on me to choose between wrestling and basketball since they are simultaneous winter sports. I chose basketball and I did whatever sport in the fall and spring that would keep me in top physical condition to play the sport I loved so much (i.e., cross country, soccer, track and field, etc.).

I took some chastisement and ridicule for going counter-culture to what seemed like the obvious choice to others, but my heart was never in wrestling the way it was in basketball. I worked my tail off and barely made the freshman squad. The following year, I was fighting the haters and the odds again, but miraculously I was given the opportunity to play with the junior varsity basketball team. Towards the end of that sophomore season, our high school was hosting the Valco League District Wrestling Tournament. The athletic director and wrestling coach begged my basketball coach to let me do both sports simultaneously because I could cover a weight class they had nobody for. You see, if you don't cover a weight class, you automatically forfeit six team points. Of course, they would like me to win, but if I could just manage to stay alive, not get pinned, or lose by a major decision, I would in essence save three team points, and that could be the difference in a slim margin of victory. So for about two weeks, I conditioned for wrestling and basketball. Ugh! They are very different, equally hard, and nearly impossible to do at the same time. It was exhausting. I did as you would expect with two weeks of training—I lost. However, I followed the game plan and sacrificed myself in such a way that we only gave up those three points as opposed to an entire six points and our team won the Valco League Districts that year.

By my junior year, the wrestling coach wanted me to spend the entire season doing both wrestling and basketball, but that would have been super difficult for me, so I chose to pursue basketball alone, provided I could qualify again. I wasn't talented enough to make varsity or start on junior varsity, but I was still given a spot on the team with another year to play the sport I loved. Unfortunately, it was a miserable season. We lost a ton, things got heated in the locker room, and bad attitudes started to sour the game I loved.

After seven years of basketball camps, summer leagues, learning a brand of basketball according to the style of the varsity high school coach, and passing all physical testing requirements, I found myself being called to the varsity basketball coach's classroom my senior year of high school. As I entered that room, I could tell by the look on my coach's face that this was going to be a tough conversation. Essentially, the coach explained that I had reached the peak of my skill level and the end of the coaching staff's room for developmental players. I was brought into that room to be told that there wasn't a jersey for me on the varsity basketball team. However, he offered me a clipboard and a whistle. He told me I had earned the respect of the coaches and my teammates for my hard work and encouragement over the years, and they would be delighted to have me coach alongside them. Unfortunately, it was devastating news to me and super embarrassing. I couldn't look my friends in the eyes and tell them I wouldn't be on the team with them. Looking back, I wasn't very mature in how I processed my emotions then. I declined the coaching gig, walked over to the wrestling coach, and asked if I could join the team. Evidently, coaches talk, and my wrestling coach actually tried to talk me out of it and suggested I stay with the basketball team in a coaching capacity, but I was too angry, hurt, and immature. So, he acquiesced to my request.

I had a moderately successful year, and our team actually won the state wrestling championship, but for me it was lonely, and I was largely bitter throughout. It turns out that physically punishing other kids in a wrestling match didn't take away the hurt deep inside—the sting of rejection and/or the reality that I simply wasn't good enough. At that moment, nothing could pacify the betrayal I felt, and angry wrestling was just exhausting. It all catches up to you at some point.

---

*I wasn't forced to leave the program;
I was just invited to a different
seat at the table and I didn't have
the wherewithal to process it.*

It took me a couple of years after high school for my hormones to level off and to get the appropriate perspective. I needed some distance from the disappointment to realize I missed an enormous opportunity to thrive in my preferred setting. While I was not good enough to make the varsity basketball team, my coaches believed I had the toolset to lead, train, encourage, and empower my peers. They wanted to give away their knowledge to me and help me learn that "coach's perspective." Rather than accepting their vantage point and their generosity to develop me on a different pathway, I elected to go another way, and find a different setting—one that I wasn't as passionate about. I should have trusted them after all of our years together and leaned into the pain. Instead, I ingested the rejection and pre-maturely ejected from the program. I wasn't forced to leave the program; I was just invited to a different seat at the table and I didn't have the wherewithal to process it. At the time, I couldn't fathom that they saw any value in me because I had a different scorecard for what was successful and valuable, and I didn't seem to check any of those boxes. I wasn't tall enough, strong enough, fast enough, or athletically talented enough, but I did understand the game. Now, in a different light, I can see they simply wanted to give me away to my best setting where I could contribute in a still meaningful way.

The right setting actually matters to all human capital. Not every city, every company, or every job within that company is made equally. There are good and bad fits. Every setting has a particular culture—"How we do things here"—and a system within that culture that demonstrates the "why" behind people's thoughts and actions. The system within that setting is so critical it will make or break the job. I've watched sports teams acquire talented players, five-star talent, and try to build a super team. Time and time again, I've watched it fail too, because they were just a collection of individuals playing selfishly. They believed their individual talent alone could carry them to victory, but they actually hindered each other (reference the NBA's Oklahoma City Thunder). I've watched other teams acquire talent but demand everyone play to a specific system and together and I've seen them bring home championships (reference the NBA's San Antonio Spurs and/or the NFL's New England Patriots). Those settings were never designed for their individual shine.

The difficult thing for highly competitive people is that they don't always see the best way forward or comprehend that they themselves may be their own biggest hurdle. When you are trained to scrap and dominate to get a roster spot on a team or win a sales contract, you channel a different level of cutthroat, "win at all costs" attitude, often in spite of the rest of the team. Many highly competitive people are so hungry, looking for a chance to prove themselves as individual contributors, that they tend to run right over others. They can be so eager and ambitious that they are blinded to what's best for the company, the team, and themselves. Like a game of musical chairs gone wrong, for the sole fact that they want to "win," they might slip into the wrong seat on the bus, putting themselves in a poor setting. Some will write off their actions as impatience, self-promotion, or ego, but truthfully, it's how competitive people tick. Competitiveness without understanding the rules of the game you are playing is a dangerous proposition. When you've spent a lifetime in that cultural river, learning to swim in a new river where you collaborate with others can be difficult. Hence, learning to discern the best setting for your contribution to the team or organization takes some outside help.

As leaders, we have three options to get our diamonds to their best destination: the best setting, where they will thrive, and where the organization will benefit as well.

RE-INVEST

Just as a CEO and team must determine what to do when their quarterly earnings exceed forecasting—pay out bonuses or put monies back into the company—so it is with their human capital. When the company is excelling, they can choose to maintain the status quo leaving everyone and everything "as is," or they can ideate and enhance the company. This may come via promoting an employee from within and/or giving increased responsibility to that employee. A business leader should regularly take inventory and determine if the best thing to do for their company and their human capital is to re-invest their skilled diamonds into their same setting or determine if another area of the company— an area that they might be even better suited for than their current role—is best. This is the diamond mining process at work.

When we begin to work with our human capital in a more meaningful and intentional way, we will begin to see each of their tangible and intangible contributions to the organization. We will not only see them doing the expected tasks of their jobs with excellence, but we will see their soft skills as well; the effect they have on their peers and customers. This collateral effect is a matter of culture. Our diamonds are culture shapers. We learn from them some best practices and micro-efficiencies to make the job better, which in turn helps company morale. With company morale high, there is better speed of service and a better attitude in the delivery of that service, which pleases the end consumer and leads to more profitability. It's difficult to quantify each of those contributions, but they are there, nonetheless.

> *When a leader ignores the proper development of their human capital, it's a loss for the diamond and the organization.*

After examining the organization's ongoing and changing needs, a leader may make one of two unwitting mistakes when they see their human capital thriving in their current assignment. They may choose to do the easy and dangerous thing, which is to do nothing at all. They don't promote the employee nor give increased responsibilities. When leaders adopt the mentality of "Leave things as is" or "If it ain't broke, don't fix it," they risk killing the zeal within their human capital and thus slowing down the momentum of the organization. Worst-case scenario, they destroy the company culture altogether. Great companies with great cultures attract great talent. Great talent doesn't want to maintain the status quo. They want personal growth, and they want to bring value-add to the overall organization. Highly competent and motivated diamonds do not like to be around mediocrity. It drags them down and kills their mental game, and there is generally insufficient execution and declining productivity levels as a result. Mediocre diamonds also don't like being around competent and motivated diamonds because it pushes them beyond their comfort level and agreement. When a leader ignores the proper development of their human capital, it's a loss for the diamond and the organization.

The second mistake a leader might make is promoting a diamond right out of their best contribution to the organization. Just because a diamond is skilled in one area or has tenure does not automatically mean the best way to incentivize them is to change their position. While a great leader understands the tension of developing their employee and getting the maximum potential out of that employee for the benefit of both the employee and the organization, sometimes the best thing a manager can do for both is to leave that diamond where they are at. The catch is that they'll need to find a different way to incentivize them. The key here is that companies should incentivize correctly for performance done correctly. While a promotion may be in order, it may not be the right incentive. So as a point of caution, do not promote people out of their best contribution to the company. That is problematic and self-defeating.

RECEIVE

The reality is that we all come to work with a pre-existing culture. We bring our work ethic, our family values, our personalities, and our expectations of a company and our co-workers with us to the job. If nobody ever received us, we would never have employment or have an opportunity to demonstrate our value-add to an organization. This may be the part that will sound most contradictory to the whole premise of the book, especially if you take everything out of context. Please don't let me lose you here. While the point of this book is to get leadership to look deeper at, invest with specificity into, and give more time and resources to the development of the human capital already under the family umbrella, I never said to avoid bringing in outside talent ever. I just believe we can do more to develop what we have, and in those instances of receiving, engrafting, and adopting outside human capital into the fold, we must infuse culture from the get-go.

I frequently caution that with each new hire from outside the "circle of trust," the onus of teaching organizational culture and enforcing accountability to that culture is on leadership, lest there be culture dilution. If leadership follows HR protocol, always uses aspirational culture as a filter for hiring practices, and clearly communicates organizational expectations up front, there is a higher chance that the diamonds received will be a proper fit. Secondly, if leadership commits to conducting regularly scheduled culture calibrations under a watchful eye from existing cultural ambassadors (i.e., stakeholders and tenured voices in an organization), then the imported addition will have their best chance of assimilation and maximum contribution. One of the subpoints of this book isn't "excluding outside talent no matter the deficit an organization may have in a particular skill set." The real emphasis is on culture curation and guarding it as you form it. Adhering to the core values and embodying the spirit behind those core values is paramount. Maintaining communication, ongoing accountability, and intentional sponsorship after employees get hired is central to the success of all current and future employees.

RELEASE

Remember, when you go to a jewelry store to look at diamonds, they all look fantastic due to the lighting. I don't mean to imply that all diamonds are alike and that imperceivable differences mean there aren't legitimate differences. Neither am I saying that one diamond with more occlusions than another diamond makes it of no value at all. I'm simply saying that all diamonds look good under the lights, and yet in different lighting, each diamond looks a different way. Therefore, we must do due diligence to see a diamond in as many lights as possible to determine its best setting and to reflect the light as it was designed to radiate. You and I might bring a really shiny diamond into our organization and realize after the fact that it may not be what we were originally looking for. It may not be the best fit for our particular setting.

While a diamond may not fit in our specific setting, I inherently believe that it will fit somewhere. If that diamond isn't a cultural fit in our organization, it needn't be personal. We should be pragmatic and mature enough to release that diamond to its best setting. The difficulty is getting the surveyor, excavator, and shaper to consider the possibility that after all the upfront investments made, in the end, the beneficiary may be someone else entirely. Knowing that truth, would one consider beginning the diamond mining process at all? This is where we have to answer the more existential questions:

1) Do we only diamond mine for personal gain or the benefit of the diamond?
2) Do we only invest in the discovery and shaping of diamonds if they will directly benefit ourselves or our organization?
3) Do we discredit and devalue a diamond if it doesn't mesh in our established setting, or do we spend even more time and resources to find the right fit?

---

*When we give the gift of the best setting
to our diamonds, everyone wins.*

If you enter into the diamond mining process, you need to begin with the premise that you are doing so with the hope of discovering, developing, and deploying each diamond into its best setting. Determining the best setting to release our diamonds begins by recognizing that our time, money, network, experience, etc. are a gift to us and we can either share it freely or hoard it. The very human capital in our care is on loan to us. In truth, nothing we have is independently/distinctly our own. Those diamonds, our human capital, ultimately don't belong to us, so it's our ethical/moral obligation to find the best setting for our human capital. They don't exist to be paraded around our necklines or flashed in our teeth. They don't exist to draw attention to us at all. They have intrinsic value, they have a larger role to play, and if they are entrusted into our care, for any amount of time, we need to give them back better than we got them. To hoard talent or hold back talent will inevitably hurt them and the organization. There needs to be a pre-determination, a resolve, to deploy that diamond to its best setting. If that diamond thrives and benefits another organization, that doesn't mean there is no credit, gratitude, or positive collateral that might come from it toward your organization. People don't forget those who freely and generously pour into them and give things away without the expectation of repayment. That is the very definition of a gift. When we give the gift of the best setting to our diamonds, everyone wins.

The caution here is that, all too often, leaders mistakenly think they can take whatever they want from their human capital because upon hire they entered into a business transaction. However, paying a salary doesn't mean a company owns the individual. It just means that human capital's rendered services are agreed to for a contracted time frame each day.

CHAPTER 5

REPRODUCING
DO IT ALL
OVER AGAIN

Growing up in Corvallis, Oregon, my babysitter was the daughter of the chief of police. She was a sweet teenage girl who took very good care of me. I got all the good snacks. I had a nice yard to play in. She even had a color TV for me to watch cartoons, which we did not have in my own home at that time. There was not much withheld from me when she watched me except this one area just off the side of the living room. Her younger brother played a gold sparkle, 5-piece Ludwig drum set. It sat in that corner, teasing me, begging to be played, but as you could imagine, I was forbidden to touch it. I was fascinated by the look of the drum shells as they sparkled under the lights, the variety of cymbals, and the pedal mechanism and foot bracing on each piece of hardware. I even loved the uniqueness of the drum throne—a leather tripod-looking setup. Hanging on the side of the floor tom was a bag of drumsticks and mallets.

Since that drum was off-limits, I would take pots, pans, milk jugs, paint buckets—pretty much anything I could gather up— and I would make them into a drum. If I wasn't banging around on that superbly designed drum kit, I was annoying my family by constantly tapping on various surfaces around the home or in the car just to hear an array of sonic goodness. Fingernail tapping on a window or flat palming the pane of glass make very different yet super fun sounds. While my parents thought I was simply "making noise," I was actually making a mental catalog and an early library of analog sound samples. In my wildest dreams, I had no idea I might ever get the chance to play real drums, let alone any other instrument.

Years later, when I was going into the sixth grade, my family and I moved to a new neighboring town—Philomath, Oregon. In this new school, we had two recesses. I wasn't going to complain because I enjoyed playing football and other games out on the playground, but I mention it because it took me the better part of the year to realize "why" we in fact had two recesses. The school blocked a second recess for those students who didn't choose an elective. It was like a glorified babysitting hour. When I inquired about these electives and where my other friends would disappear to, I learned they went to "band class." I didn't even know our school had a band class. I wanted to be in the band.

After I spoke to my friends and the band teacher about the details of this newly discovered elective, I had to go home and ask my parents if I could sign up for band class. While I had no actual professional percussive instrument, I learned that we could actually rent a snare drum from the local music store. As you might imagine, they were not particularly excited about my choice of instrument, but they conceded. I jumped in full force, enthusiastically learning different time signatures, various sticking patterns, and how to count an ungodly amount of measures simply to play one triangle hit in an orchestral piece. If you know, you know. I finished out my sixth-grade year tapping out the galloping rhythms of the "William Tell Overture" and buzz-rolling the intro music from "21st Century Fox" on my snare. Although in my heart of hearts—that heart that loved 80s glam rock—I dreamed of playing a full drum set.

Up to that point, I had never sat on a drum set. The only one I had seen up close I was forbidden to touch. That is when I learned about jazz band. As seventh grade was beginning, I learned from my classmates that if I made the middle school jazz band, I would get to play on a full drum set instead of just the orchestral percussion instruments like timpani or the dreaded bells. Unfortunately, you need to actually practice on a drum set to audition on a drum set, so you can get more time on a drum set. The system was against me. Once again, I found myself in the position of asking my parents for something they were still not overly excited about. I wanted to upgrade from my lonely snare drum rental to a full drum set. Rightfully so, they said it was too expensive and that they weren't sure they wanted to make that kind of financial investment to begin with. They had valid reasons for their reluctance considering my older brothers had all begun some instrument with much enthusiasm but then failed to practice and eventually quit. They just didn't want to make the investment to begin with. Being resourceful, I found an older drum set with no hardware stuffed way back in the band closet, and I begged the band teacher to let me take those beat-up drum shells home so that I could combine them with my snare rental. I thought maybe, just maybe, I'd get decent enough on that old piece of junk to make the jazz band. My band teacher acquiesced.

Eventually, I did make the jazz band, but I encountered another hurdle. I thought learning music and playing with proficiency would be my biggest lesson, but in reality, I didn't even know the basics of how to assemble or disassemble the hardware on an actual drum set. The Frankenstein I was beating on was drum shells only. I had no idea how to extend and condense the hardware to the proper length. I didn't know how to get the appropriate angle for the cymbals. In jazz competitions, there is generally one shared drum set and the hardware might be set to different heights and positions depending on the height of the drummer who played just before you. There is very little turnaround time in the transition between school bands, so I needed help. Fortunately, I had drumming classmates in the grades ahead of me who were extremely knowledgeable, patient, and saw potential in me. They felt it was worth their time to invest in me. I learned how to not only play my instrument but how to care for it. I also learned the value of teaching others what I had learned, fostering a culture of "paying it forward."

I did finally talk my parents into buying a drum set of my own, with the agreement that I would play in the school band until I graduated from high school. That six-year commitment might have intimidated another kid, but for me, it was a no-brainer. As I got older, I played in pep bands, orchestras, and jazz bands. I even played in some side trios and accompanied some local playwrights in the local theater. However, with each opportunity afforded me, I realized my time in school was passing and there was a new, upcoming wave of percussionists ready to learn too.

It is in this reality that I formed a mantra, a belief system—my "why"—in regard to perpetuating talent, even at the expense of my own opportunities.

However, to be a first-chair musician in my school of thinking, you need to be able to teach what you know to others and reproduce who you are.

In a band, you have chairs. Chairs are essentially classifications or rankings of instrumental proficiency, leadership potential, and more. If you were first chair, you were expected to sight-read music cold turkey and play it pretty accurately. First chairs generally got first pick of solos and instrument choice and they often assigned out the other parts to the section. While that is the traditional expectation of a first-chair musician, my experience with great band peers and music teachers shaped a new paradigm for me. In my opinion, a second-chair musician should be able to do what a traditional first-chair does. They should be fluent in sight-reading music, learning and writing out parts, handling complex solos, etc. They should be able to assist their section as required. However, to be a first-chair musician in my school of thinking, you need to be able to teach what you know to others and reproduce who you are.

REASON

Reproduction is an essential piece to keeping all things moving forward in life. This moving forward means nothing stays in a static state but is perpetually and dynamically progressing. There is a beginning, but there is also an end. This applies to all of us and to the things that we give ourselves to. There is a natural life cycle that cannot be circumvented or denied. It is inevitable and it is a fact. It is this finite reality that ought to keep us sober and focused as to "why" we do what we do.

As a musician, I understand there are an array of reasons behind how we start our musical journey, the choices we make along the way, and the impact and/or legacy we may intentionally or unintentionally leave behind. Most musicians simply want to share their art with the world. Some love to share that art from their contribution to the sound studio—innovating, recording, and tweaking things until they have something worth sharing. Some musicians reluctantly do studio songwriting sessions but prefer the adrenaline rush of sharing their art from the stage. Both avenues can leave a musician longing for something more. When a musician records new music, they must go out and perform that music. After the tour, they are expected to create fresh content, so they find themselves back in the studio. It's cyclical.

When a musician performs on stage, all they have is the audience's applause after their set. After the emotions die down, there is nothing but a fading memory. The very next day, they start from scratch and the whole process repeats itself. City after city, dive bar or stadium, they must "bring it" every single night to receive that applause. Each night will end just like the one before.

What begins as new and exciting, possibly a dream fulfilled, soon becomes routine and bland. To get out of this endless cycle or at least to have more meaning to what you are doing, you need a deeper reason than the one you may have initially started with. If you and I don't want to merely perform for applause and a fleeting high, we must find ways to give back, elevate those around us, and teach them to do the same. The real magic, the gift, will never be the experiences alone, although they make for great stories. It won't be the applause, because that never lasts long enough to do much with it. It simply comes on and then disappears like a vapor. It shouldn't be the paycheck alone, although that is a nice consolation prize. The real win is that you have a talent to share art with the world, an art you can do solo and/or collaborate with others on, and the ability to share your knowledge around that art with someone else so they might do the same—not simply sharing the art, but the reproductive reasonings behind it all.

If we live that short-sighted and selfishly, we will watch wisdom and flourishing fade from our lives as quickly as applause.

The reason for this book and this process is that I believe that the Diamond Mining mentality is superior to that of a common Jewelry Thief. It is an intentional and repeatable process of discovering, developing, and deploying and it needs to be reproduced to have sustainability and longevity generation after generation. Without the final step of intentionally reproducing, we are just going to go through the motions in life, leaving untouched and/or underdeveloped human capital in our wake. If we live that short-sighted and selfishly, we will watch wisdom and flourishing fade from our lives as quickly as applause. Reproduction at scale is demonstrated when leaders actively and consistently follow this process and then invite the human capital they poured into to do the same. Eventually, this will be normative and cultural in the family and/or organization.

We all have a reason for doing the things that we do. Good, bad, or indifferent, we have an impetus for our behaviors. Reproduction is no different. Reproducing yourself, your methods, your shortcuts, your tricks, your best practices, and your attitude is one thing, but reproducing your "why" is wholly another. There has to be a clear "why" for you to put in the effort in the first place, and you definitely will need a "why" to stay in the fight. This is Reproductive Culture 101.

I have a desire to elevate the lives of people around me, especially those who are coming behind me. I want to help them find their best contribution to their family, their work, and ultimately to the world. While that is reason enough for me to make intentional investments and necessary sacrifices, my larger goal is teaching those people the reason behind the Diamond Mining process and convincing them of the necessity to not only adopt it but to teach it to others.

RISK

While the reproductive process is essential to life and growth, there are no guarantees that it will come without trial. Aside from the herculean physical effort and pain involved, there are plenty of other complications and known risks when it comes to reproduction. Some struggle with infertility. Some suffer a miscarriage or stillbirth. Some babies are breech and require a C-section to be extracted from the womb. Despite these known factors, many women will testify that childbearing is a joy and worthwhile. So, it is with the Diamond Mining process.

Leaders assume a great deal of risk when caring and providing for others. A mom sacrifices sleep and food for her children. A father sacrifices time with his family when traveling for work. A businesswoman thinks about each of her employee's families when she is making tough decisions. These are not new concepts. However, there is risk on the other side, too. Those who seek us out for teaching, for mentoring, or who we invite into a discipleship experience are taking some calculated risks. Let me explain something I picked up from Dr. Daniel Brown's "Raising More Leaders within Your Church" sermon series.

When people follow you:

They actually believe you know where you are going.

They actually believe where you are going is where they should go.

Note: It is normal for people to get on and off the bus. In a masterclass from the Sam Chand Leadership Institute, Chand says, "Those you start with may not be the ones you finish with."

They actually believe you will succeed in getting them to where they are going.

They actually believe you won't do to them what other leadership has done to them.

This is not a dictatorship nor is it a matter of subservience and control. Rather this is about voluntary submission and trust. This is about believing that what someone else has or knows is worth receiving and being reproduced in yourself and others. This risk is predicated on the joy of reward.

REWARD

After high school, I thought I was going to be a rockstar, traveling the United States and possibly one day I would do some international tours. I had been drumming since the sixth grade and picked up a few other instruments along the way. I was eager to launch out there and share my art with the world. Unfortunately, that is NOT at all what happened. I broke up with my high school band, dropped out of art school in Oregon, and took a completely different life trajectory in Southern California. While off in California, I made a few failed attempts trying out for some local Los Angeles bands who already had signed contracts. My drum skills were not quite at the level necessary for those established professionals. It was disappointing because I enjoyed their music and would have loved playing live with them, but it was not paralyzing. I simply looked for my best fit to contribute because I knew I had something to offer. While it wasn't likely to transpire in the arena or in the manner in which I had originally estimated it might, I was still going to find my setting. Not thinking too much of my dream of stage performance, I turned my attention towards the classroom and began teaching music lessons. I started out pretty basic and not overly confident, but the more I did it the better I got. I tweaked lesson plans and tried to make them interactive and fun. I helped develop musicians for school bands, garage bands, and different faith communities' praise bands. I even used my broken Spanish to work bilingually in those same spaces. Before I knew it, I was getting invited to travel and teach on the subjects of music and leadership development. Never in my wildest dreams did I think I would travel the world as a music teacher of sorts. Along the way, I got to jam with some great musicians, some more well-known than others, but all very gifted. I have taught students who have gone on to professional music careers and others I just introduced to the love of the instrument. I applied the Diamond Mining process to my musical instruction too. I taught all my students to teach what they know and reproduce who they are so they can make money at something they love, and also so that they might multiply their love of music in others. All in all, I got to travel abroad, make new friends, record music, and reproduce much of what was deposited in me as young human capital back in little Philomath, Oregon. What a rich reward.

If you and I believe something was worth doing once, would we not consider doing it again and again?

A common question people ask themselves in retrospect is "If I could do it all over again, would I?" Secondly, "What would I change?" If you and I believe something was worth doing once, would we not consider doing it again and again? Sure, we might find ways to do it better, but we would still value it, right? This is the idea behind reproduction. The Diamond Mining process places a premium on the human capital in our care and the need to reproduce this ideology in others. It is intentional and nuanced, but super doable and replicable. There is a valid reason and clear risk and reward at play, but the alternative choice of Jewelry Thief is definitely not preferred. Although the Diamond Mining process takes time, effort, and great expenditure, it also brings great joy to everyone involved. The payout is much larger than most of us can anticipate. It's not simply personal satisfaction, but there is a joy, a dream, and a pathway forward for the human capital in our care. It is much like raising children. You think you are caring for them for eighteen years and then sending them off to college, only to realize they come back and still need your money and wisdom. Then they get married, have children of their own, and you find yourself in marriage counseling, grandparenting, and doing the whole thing all over again. It's just like that; you're never quite finished. Yet, when we see our children adulting and their children being productive members of society, there is a deep satisfaction within and a knowing that they will teach the next generation even more.

That is worth reproducing.

CONCLUSION

ell, that was a much shorter read than you thought it was going to be, huh?!

You're welcome.

The goal of the book was to give you practical examples that you could execute immediately. It was outlined to be brief, be bright, and be gone. It has been my experience that people who don't quite know as much about a subject as they may lead you to believe tend to ramble on and on. I know this from first-hand experience as I've seen my fair share of eyes roll into the back of heads and drool slip out of the sides of my audience's mouths as I speak. I'd rather leave y'all longing than loathing. My goal with this book was to articulate something succinct and to the point. Something less theoretical and more prescriptive in nature. I do believe that it is both a timely and urgent message, as it has been ignored for far too long in the home, in the marketplace, and in various faith communities.

Metaphorically, I know I packed three oversized suitcases of truth into a small carry-on bag. Good luck getting that past your very own mental TSA agents (i.e., cynicism and pride). I will leave it to you and your team to do the unpacking. Better yet, get the master class and/or invite me to dialogue with you and your team. Together, we can wrestle through the five steps in the Diamond Mining process, and we can dig into some of the more nuanced specifics of each. The process itself is not overly complex, it just requires intentionality and consistency. The Diamond Mining process will just expose to a large degree what you value, what you'll pay for those values, and if you believe others should have access to and consider reproducing those same values. In my opinion, our human capital will always be our most important asset, and we need to do better with them. I write this book and share these tips so that they not only experience a healthier, more intentional home and/or work environment but so that they will curate this culture in their own lives and future businesses and replicate it wherever they go. If we each begin to do our part now, this can scale for the benefit of all.

I said at the beginning of this book that if you follow the five steps in the Diamond Mining process, you will begin to see potential where you didn't see it before, you will recognize the value and costly investment to bring forth that potential in another, you will gain insight into ways to develop that human capital with specificity, and you will discern your motives in all of this. I hope I made good on that statement.

Now go mine some diamonds and help them find their best setting, so they can fully reflect what has been uniquely placed inside of them, waiting to be shared with the world.

Milton Keynes UK
Ingram Content Group UK Ltd.
UKHW021104200324
439767UK00016B/652